C000181438

Aff

Alphabet

By Rosemary Arti

Affirmation Alphabet

First published 2021

Copyright©2021 Rosemary Arti

First Printed in United Kingdom 2021

Published by Conscious Dreams Publishing
www.consciousdreamspublishing.com

Edited by Elise Abram

Typeset by Oksana Kosovan

ISBN: 978-1-913674-80-9

Dedication

Dedicated to Isabella, who is always an inspiration. I love you x

Message from the Author
Rosemary Arti

This little book contains nuggets of wisdom I have learnt on this fantastic journey of life.

The original version of this book, which was penned several years ago, was a very different creation to what we have here today. The initial idea came about after watching a television programme on teenage pregnancy. There was one young lady who drew my attention. She was preparing for the birth of her child. I was in awe at how organised and emotionally grounded she was, especially since she was so young and facing the enormous responsibility of getting ready to bring new life into this world.

She had got together all the items needed for the arrival of a newborn, and had organised everything beautifully for her unborn child. The next thing that struck me was the way she spoke about leaving a legacy for her child. She had wanted, and indeed needed, her child to know that he/she was loved very much, and had written a love letter to her unborn child. This struck a deep chord within me. It made me begin to think of what I would have wanted to hear and the things I would have wanted to know as a young girl growing up.

When I watched the programme, I had not long given birth to my youngest child, my only daughter. And as I thought about what I would have wanted to have heard, and how I would have wanted to feel loved, as a young girl, I began a love letter to my daughter, but also, I believe, to myself. My inner child. I began to write affirmations for every letter of the alphabet, and *Affirmation Alphabet* was born.

There have been a couple of heartfelt versions of *Affirmation Alphabet* over the years, and although they were a little rudimentary in their infancy, the seeds planted then are now the product of what has been developed into what we have here today. Through all the twists and turns, ups and downs, highs and lows, I am here, now.

My hope is that this little road map for the journey will touch someone.

Love and light

Rosie x

~ A ~

Abundant Affirmations

The consistent, running narrative we play in our heads, be they negative or positive, are affirmations we bring to life with the power of belief. Over time, we can make the conscious decision to unlearn narratives we find unproductive and, quite frankly, useless to who we authentically are. In doing so, we can retrain our minds and mentally reinforce positive beliefs.

When we are born, actually, before we are born, the narrative starts, and subject to our demographics, this narrative will be wide and vast and just as hard to quantify. Just look at the world we inhabit, and all that goes on in and around it.

And so, it begins – everyone's story. The long and short of it is that we tend to believe what we are taught as children by those who care for us or who are in authoritative positions be it siblings, educators or the media. Unfortunately, a lot of what we are taught to believe are false truths.

Our minds are like the hard drive of a computer. It receives and stores information for later use. This information and programming can then be called upon to respond to life situations. It becomes like a default button. So, in saying this, when we look at the traditional ways we were brought up, it is usually a baton-passing exercise from those that came before.

This would be great, excellent even, if the information from the start did not get so twisted and misused for egoic madness. The ego has needs ... bless. It strives to keep itself alive, and this is achieved through many different avenues. The key to this mission is our minds.

The mind is merely another tool in the arsenal we are given to explore our life here on earth. Along with our bodies and all the wonderful things they can do, we have the mind as the main control processing unit.

So, inadvertently, the thoughts our minds are attuned to, and the belief in the thoughts we generate, will dictate what kind of outcome we are going to achieve. Therefore, it is simple really – we need to retune our hard drives, our minds, with positive truth about who we REALLY are.

We should not get into the habit of accepting others' limited views of who we are, and what we can achieve. Remember, we each see and interpret the world around us from our own, unique perspective, and each of us will view life through our own awareness. We are not here to live our lives through the limited perceptions of how we see each other.

Here is an example of an affirmation I would write in my diary:

'I AM MENTALLY AND PHYSICALLY FIT AND HEALTHY, FROM THE VERY TIP OF MY HEAD TO THE VERY SOLES OF MY FEET. ALL THAT IS WITHIN ME AND THAT SURROUNDS ME IS PURE LOVE AND LIGHT. I AM FINANCIALLY STABLE AND SECURE, TO ENJOY AND LIVE MY BEST LIFE EVER ... THANK YOU.'

So, tribe, let's start bigging ourselves up!

~ B ~

Beautifully Bold

They say beauty is in the eye of the beholder. As the beholden, we can look further than the superficial, look a little deeper, at that which is within us. There is a beauty that lies deep within us all and is mirrored to those around us. Fundamentally, all of nature, all of us, are created from this same beautiful source. So we all share this beautiful DNA.

It is important we recognise that we are more than what we physically see. There is an essence that every living thing possesses. This source, spirit, soul – whatever turn of phrase we may use to describe it – lies within us all, as pure energy. It is like that feeling we get when we are pulled to someone for some unknown reason; we just feel a connect.

That is energy, like a magnet operating in a magnetic field.

All of nature shares this beauty. This amazing energy. We, as humans, hold this inner, beautiful, light-filled energy. When we arrive at the realisation of this, we release within ourselves a sense of this inner power. We begin to radiate this magical, internal energy and pass it on to others. In turn, we attract even more of this dynamic and powerful energy. This inner state, this ball of life-giving energy, grows stronger and more powerful the more it is exercised. The more life-affirming we become, the stronger and bolder our presence will be.

We must never be afraid to show our beauty. We should not 'downsize' on who we authentically are to make others feel comfortable, just because they are unable to accept our radiance and our inner glow.

We should not shrink who we are for those who are happier for us to stay living at a level that does not disturb or upset the status quo of their life. There may be times when we must come to an awareness there may be those among us who are not yet in a place to consciously receive who we authentically are, and that's okay. It is a little like trying to pour a litre of water into a very small glass. They just will not have the capacity to hold what it is you must give and, to be honest, they are just not ready for you yet!

In so saying, we will come across people who feel they do not have the capability to understand or appreciate who you are, and they may be afraid of digging deeper into their own self and discovering things they may not wish to deal with. It could come in the form of resentment because they are yet to attain a level of consciousness or awareness that others have reached. Or it could simply be they are afraid to release their very own power, and where it could lead them.

Whatever the reason, this is not our business. Our business is taking care of our own self. When we become aware of who we really are, and when we step into who we were authentically designed to be, we are then ready to flourish, spread our metaphorical wings and stand beautifully bold in who we are. Remember, although we are all connected, we are also unique in what we bring to the world.

We are human BEINGS, not human doings. Let us consider not following the status quo, and living our lives, through the 'blind leading the blind' mentality. We are here to create new status quos, to find and experience evolving new ways to consciously move forward. So, let us open our eyes and our hearts, be honest with ourselves, forgive ourselves, forgive those that we need to forgive, and move forward, as we discover our beautiful inner self, and step boldly into the beauty life has to offer us, and what we can beautifully give to the world.

~ C ~

Conscious Curiosity

We all have deep-rooted beliefs that have been passed on – given to, thrown at, indoctrinated – from a very early age. Whether we choose to believe it or not, there will be thousands upon thousands of pieces of information we have stored in our subconscious.

Our thought patterns and our actions often stem from these subconscious pieces of information that we store away and retrieve whenever needed. The infamous default buttons.

When thought patterns come to me that hold a degree of negativity, I have to consciously stop myself and question it. Where is this really coming from? Is there any truth in the thought? Is it a productive thought? Why am I thinking in this way?

When we begin to question ourselves, our thoughts, our behaviour, we open up a level of consciousness that helps us to look deeper. If we are still enough in the moment, and quiet enough to hear, our consciousness will give us the answers we are ultimately searching for.

It's like a satnav system in a car: you program it with an address, and it will search for the best possible route for you to complete your journey. Well, heads up people – we have one of those for ourselves, for human beings! It is called your gut, your instinct, your nose. Whatever you call it, you have it, okay?

When you begin to question yourself, as to why you think the way you think, and what prompts you to take certain actions, you open up the subconscious and begin to see and understand yourself on a more conscious level.

When we begin to ask questions of ourselves on this more conscious level, it helps us to redress and rewire untruths we have kept dormant in our subconscious minds. When we are operating from a subconscious that has not been checked for 'viruses', we are then operating on an unconscious level, and if you are unconscious, you cannot really be living, can you?

Once you get into this habit of stopping for a moment to question the source of your thought or action, it becomes a lot easier to recognise and, soon enough, you will just be existing from a clearer, more conscious perspective. In turn, this will help you to make clearer, more concise, and ultimately more positive decisions for yourself.

You are your own project to work on. Give yourself the time and the space that you undoubtedly give to everything and everyone else around you, that ensures their shit runs smoothly. You are the best person for the job of looking after you.

Circumstances, feelings, emotions, the environment, what or whoever it is, can and will change, constantly. The one thing that will remain and stay in place and be static, so to speak, and will always be with you, is YOU. Be curious about yourself and start discovering who you really are, and enjoy the process!

~ D ~

Divine Destiny

When you dare to dream, where do you go to? What do you desire to experience? What is it that desire to learn? There is something deep within all of us that yearns for some 'thing' and, often, this 'something' seems elusive to us.

We all have within us a divine destiny. An inner navigation system, if you like, that has our true destinies already mapped out for us. Divinely, we get to choose how we are going to travel through this road of life. It is here where our choices come into play, and help us navigate through this beautiful, wonderful world we inhabit.

There will be times when we are unable to make certain choices for ourselves, due to our life situations. These are just what they are: life situations, events that take place 'outside' of us. These life situations may, and usually do, have a hand at moulding us somewhat, into who we are but, fundamentally, 'situations' are not *who we are*.

We all hold an extraordinary power, and it is when we come to the realisation that no matter what is happening around us in situations external to our beings, we all have the capacity and capability to control our minds to be fully connected, and at the same time detached from what it is that may be occurring around us. In so doing, this allows the essence of our inner selves to guide us, rather than us defaulting to using only our minds to take charge and lead the ship.

Being detached does not mean we are cold and uncaring. In contrast, it is the complete opposite. Not allowing the mind to engage with its own 'storytelling' and getting into our feelings, allowing ourselves to look at a situation with no background or backdrop, allows our level of consciousness to rise. We are then not reacting or responding from the automatic 'default button' of our subconscious.

This, in turn, gives our inner self space to breathe. This 'space' lets us know everything is going to be all right. We are going to be all right. We can then make a pact with ourselves (our mind and our inner self) to say, "Yes, we've got this together, and every little thing will be all right."

~ E ~

Energy

We are all created from a great source of energy. We all contain this wonderful energy that we were made from. We emit energy. We are all just, simply, energy.

Our energy will fluctuate from one moment to the next, depending on our current situation. Remembering that we control the power in how we engage in any given situation, we can readily come to the table, so to speak, with positive, conscious energy.

We also need to be mindful of those that may be deemed 'energy vampires', who can suck all our energy reserves and leave us feeling totally spent because, through no conscious thought of their own, they have the need to retell victim stories and convince us the world 'is out to get you' and life is full of doom and gloom. Do not entertain – *#keepitmoving*.

You may have two people in identical circumstances, with identical demographics, etc. Everything is the same. Person one will see all the obstacles they will have to overcome to reach a place they feel is their peace. They will tell themselves stories in which they have the leading role, and in which they are the victim, and that all around them have hindered their very existence (This may be slightly exaggerated here, but I want you to get the drift of what I am trying to convey). The energy level of person one is not going to be great, is it? Batteries will be running on low. Choices may, and often do, become clouded. They may begin to suffer with illnesses. All this negative energy has an impact and causes imbalances within us.

On the other hand, person two looks at the situation and sees what they can achieve and sets about making it happen, rather than getting emotionally caught up and telling themselves stories about the things they cannot do anything about, not having to involve anyone in their story, or minding and relaying the business of someone else's story.

They will metaphorically and mentally roll up their sleeves and get on with getting on. They flow along, and feel at peace within themselves, because they have made mental choices with inner self guidance, for what is best for the whole self. Holistic care.

This produces a balanced energy that allows them to make clearer, more conscious choices. This ultimately creates positive energy, from the inside out. Go out and be electrifying (not literally – you know what I mean).

~ F ~

Fearless Faith

Faith has nothing to do with religion (in my humble opinion).

When we begin to encompass who we are, this confidence that inner self gifts us, the knowledge of power that we hold, this releases a powerful sense of peace within us. All these wonderful things come from a place where an inner faith resides; a place that simply 'knows'.

With this faith, we know that regardless of what our life situation looks like on the outside and whatever the circumstances we may find ourselves in, we can hold on to this deep-rooted, uncompromising, fearless faith, because ultimately what we see physically and from whatever perspective is not all that there is to this life.

Our faith gives us the courage to go on this roller coaster journey called life, and experience all that it has to offer. Our faith helps us to ride the highs and hold on tight when we go through the lows, and having faith helps us to remember that no matter what the ride, everything will be okay.

We have undoubtedly experienced situations in which we can see no way out, and we then call to a place deep inside ourselves for help, "Just this once, please, I need help." And when you believe, truly believe with conviction that there is more to this life than we can physically see, the Universe will always lend you a hand.

Get in the habit of exercising fearless faith. When everyone around you *tries* to tell you all the reasons that you cannot do something, smile and let them entertain their own narrative. What they think is none of your business, anyway. You and faith go have a one-to-one, then show the dream slayers how faith works.

~ *G* ~

Grateful

It is important that we show gratitude as we go along this life road. Connectiveness can be lost when we forget to take a moment to be thankful for anything positive. It can simply be a quiet word in your head, a journal or diary entry. It can even be an elaborate ceremony of thanks. Whatever way you feel is right for you will not matter. What really matters is the acknowledgement.

When I was younger, we were taught to say 'grace' before eating a meal, not really understanding it, rather just doing it because we were told to. Ahh, but now, I recognise. I recognise all the wonderful things in this life here, this life now, that I am grateful for. It could be the simplest of things. The transport system that gets me to work, in all kinds of weather, and with the current world situation, in all kinds of circumstances as well. I Am Grateful.

For example, there may be a time that you miss your bus for work one morning, and initially start to 'get into your feelings' about it, only later to discover that said bus had been caught up in some sort of accident, and passengers were injured. Grateful. Just saying. There will be times that we think or believe that we are receiving the short end of the stick but, in reality, it is a blessing in disguise. Be thankful.

I often lift up a thank you for the ingredients I am using in a dish. As I prepare them, I say thank you, as gratitude to the hands that have planted, tended, picked and packed said ingredients, and for these ingredients to be made readily available for me to use as nutrition for my body.

When I look at nature I am grateful for the processes that allow carbon dioxide to be made into oxygen so we can breathe and stay alive. When I feel the sun on my face, I feel grateful for its warmth. When I hear a baby laughing, I am grateful that I am designed to hear this beautiful sound. The list is endless.

Gratitude can come in many forms and is a simple way to pass forward some positive energy. We can also be grateful for experiences in our lives that may not have been positive, but we can be grateful for the lesson that experience may have taught us. Gratitude always, for the lessons and the blessings.

~ H ~

Happy Hopes

When things around us are not going great, or our life situation is not what or where we really want it to be, it can be easy to feel disheartened. It is at these times we need to dig deep and find our 'happy place', wherever that may be.

For myself, I tend to see myself on a beautiful white sand beach, with big, whitewashed waves on the horizon, propelling high over the teal-coloured sea, creating crashing crests that form around my feet in the warm sand. The sun kisses my skin, and in turn my skin drinks in the warmth and the energy from this solar connection. Ahh … happy place. I am instantly smiling. This is my hope; that I will someday live somewhere where I am surrounded and connected to nature in some form.

We all have hopes for our lives; hope for all good things, for a bright future, good health and well-being. Hopes for our family and friends. Hope, hope, hope. Hope is another way, as I see it, of exercising faith. Faith is fundamentally the *hope* of things that we cannot see; a complete blind trust or confidence in someone or something. So, I guess hope and faith go hand in hand. Our hopes are embedded in faith, and that faith resides at the centre of our very being.

~ I ~

Intuition, Intuition, Intuition

What can I say about this mega-tool in our arsenal – intuition? It is there, that is for sure; that gut feeling we all experience. That feeling that says to you: don't turn left here, go right instead. You don't know why, but 'something' speaks to you to do it. That gut feeling that emerges when we are placed in dangerous situations. Your mind will make an assessment, and then physiology will kick in, and your body will follow suit and respond in either a fight or flight mode.

Our intuition, our gut, is our internal satnav system, which I spoke about earlier. We have been equipped to handle any situation we may find ourselves in. Trouble is, we have become lazy, and tend not to do too much thinking for ourselves. We have become dependent on others telling us what to do and how to do it and that, in turn, quietens our natural instincts and our intuition becomes dulled.

When we become curious about our very selves, there is something that begins to awake inside of us. It's like a sleeping giant that slowly starts to rouse. Intuition gives way for this natural curiosity to be opened up even further, and for us to delve deeper, and to consciously discover for our own selves more of the power of who we are and the vastness of what we are truly about. Do not just follow the mind; that can and will tell all kinds of stories, and we know half that shit isn't real. Follow the gut. The gut just knows.

~ J ~
Joy

When we are truly free in mind, conscious enough of 'the' moment right now, there is this overwhelming release within the body. A sensation that fills us fully; a deep swirling and swelling. I call this sensational bliss, pure joy.

We can experience this sensation at any time. We do not need to wait for a situation to arise, or an event to occur, for us to embrace this natural high. We can choose to be in that place whenever we wish.

For myself, when I am feeling overwhelmed by a situation, or self-talk starts telling 'stories' and begins the process again of creating a negative space within me, I stop. I acknowledge the thought, or the given situation, take a breath, remember that all of whatever 'this' *is* happens outside of me, and is *not* me. Repeat: this is *not* me.

I can then let that which *is* me, my *inner self*, make the conscious choice to not be attached to whatever it is, although I am always fully connected. This is when the magic happens. This is when an overwhelming sense of peace fills the spaces, where the breath has released all that which is not needed or indeed required. This space is filled with a calming, caressing sense of stillness.

Our very breath brings us joy, if we can just stop for a moment to breathe, really breathe. When we feel balanced, we naturally feel good. Our energy levels are positive, and in turn that attracts positivity. We make clearer and more conscious choices.

As we begin to develop this habit, we want to engage with it even more. We want to continue to experience this inner happy, this inner joy. Undoubtedly, what we are feeling and experiencing on the inside radiates outwards, like osmosis, permeating and penetrating, until it just bursts out, like a beautiful ray of light.

~ K ~

Kismet

We are an original, conscious thought that came into being through the pure manifestation of that original, conscious thought. We were predestined.

I know it's a lot to get our heads around but, honestly, that is the truth as I see it. Not everyone will agree, and to be fair, I wouldn't expect everyone to. In fact, I believe I would be quite taken aback, shocked even, as I know the majority of us human beings are actually playing at being human *doings*, and operate from only a partial level of consciousness, and just will not be able to relate to what I am saying, and that's fine.

We were preordained for our lives here, right now, on this earth. I don't think we had a choice in that, but we do have a choice in how we go through and live this life we have been graciously gifted. When we align ourselves to this concept, and stop resisting life, and learn the skill of 'flowing' instead of resistance, we begin to merge, blend, melt into our true nature and this, in turn, makes our journey more palpable.

When we go with the flow of life, everything becomes easier. In so saying, I know that shit happens. There is stuff happening all the time, all around us, that is not so great. However, what helps us to navigate these life situations that undoubtedly will occur is our mindset, and how we choose to be in every moment we have been given.

It is what it is. Whatever it is, we have a choice in how we live it.

~ *L* ~

Love and Light

Our very essence is that of pure love and light. This is our rocket fuel, our lifeline. Just as blood flows through the veins and arteries, so does this love and light flow through us. There are those of us who radiate this vibrant, glowing, magnetic energy, and this will be very evident when you encounter it.

There are those of us, due to past traumas of varying and vast complexities, who do not emit this brilliant radiance and, for whatever reason, choose to stay closed off, technically, from self. We withhold this love from ourselves. We choose not to let the light within us shine.

Well, it's a good job that this love and light that resides deep within us is not going anywhere, and we can all make conscious choices to awaken that which may have been dulled within us. This essence, this source, may have been duped into remission, but never submission.

Love ultimately is what makes the world go around, and we firstly need to learn and understand this resource of self-love for our own self. We need to nurture and grow to develop our very own sense of the magic that is self-love. When we respect and appreciate this love we have for ourselves, we are well equipped to go into the world and LOVE, LOVE, LOVE.

~ M ~

Majesty

When we begin to look closer, to consider and to become more consciously aware of who we truly are, the reality is majestic. We are majestic beings, created from a majestic source. We are majesty, inherently. It is in our DNA.

At this point, I would like to put it out there, for the record and the naysayers, that there is no 'lane' that I will be staying in. There may be 'lanes' that have been designed for me to stay in, but I am not here to appease, or live my life through the limitations or confines of any other. I am not here to make you feel comfortable in keeping the status quo. There will be no 'stay in your lane' for me. I am the lane. I AM MY OWN LANE. Straight.

You know, it may be hard for others to comprehend this majesty. This inner, regal nobility that we possess, that we harness, that belongs solely to us. No one can take this away from us. Some may be perplexed into thinking, how? How can they, who seemingly have nothing to offer in this world, nothing to show, *materially*, be so confident in who they are? They have nothing.

Ahh, the sweetness of this. To the outside world, or rather, to those that operate from a certain level of limited consciousness, there is a belief that those who may be materially poor and might not be worthy of greatness, should not be happy. 'Why are poor people so freaking happy?' What their unconscious minds have yet to reveal to those who believe themselves to be better than anyone else due to material wealth, educational status, or status in general, is that, yes, they may be materially poor, but they are so very spiritually rich.

This perception comes from what you choose to believe is true. Some of us will only believe what the eyes can physically see, and can only really see things from this level of perception. It is a blinkered viewpoint that lies deep within the subconscious, that may never get checked for trojans or viruses. Their peripheral view is only what they can see directly in front of their own eyes. No more, no less.

Those of us with a different understanding, and may operate from a different level of consciousness, see far more deeply and widely than this. We know that there is more to life than what actually meets the eye. There is a grounded, fundamental sense of I AM that cannot be shifted or shaken, regardless of what is said about you, how others 'feel' about you, whatever is going on around you, what others try to 'do' to you, etc. None of those external 'things' matter because, deep down, you know you have been sourced and created by an omnipresence so great, so vast, so majestic.

~ N ~

Nice

There is no cost afforded to being nice. It's free, and every human being has access. Being nice, just to be nice to another, without wanting or expecting anything in return, is surely a good thing. Just be nice for the sake of being nice. In turn, this energy that you put forward will bless someone else. Nonetheless, these blessings do come back to you, directly or indirectly.

When someone is genuinely nice to us, and shows kindness, without wanting anything in return, we feel good. It can also be quite humbling when another goes out of their way to show us an act of kindness. It helps us to remember that we are all, collectively, one big family.

Kindness should not be saved for only those who are within our 'inner circle', or those we think 'deserve' our kindness. We can get into the habit of showing kindness wherever we are, and with whomever we may encounter. It could be holding a door open for the person behind you. It could be smiling at a stranger. It could be helping someone get onto a bus, who may be having difficulties. It could even be paying for someone's grocery shopping at the supermarket.

The more acts of kindness you promote, the more you have an urge, a drive, to be nice, to be kind. Remember, in so doing, you need to be nice and kind to yourself, also. This can be achieved in the form of self-care, and genuinely looking after yourself holistically. When you are nice to 'self', you are taking care of all your being – mind, body, and soul. Just be nice. Please.

~ O ~

Omnipetent

We are beings that have been created through the power of omnificence; an all knowing, all powerful force. There is, then, a level of omnipotence within us all; as all things have originated from this same source.

To acknowledge that we all contain this mega-source of indestructible and eternal energy is mind-blowing and, yes, it should blow our minds. It should blow our minds of any hard-wired untruths that we have adopted as beliefs.

Over time, our minds have been imprinted with fears, insecurities, false truths about who we truly are, and why we are here. Yes, these hard-wired ideals that do not align with who we are, and our greater self, need to be blown out of the window, to make space for real truth; the truth about human beings and what we really are.

When we begin to strip away those things that are external to our being, and begin to look within ourselves, we start to see our lives on a whole new level. When we begin to understand that we are not identified as any label that anyone has put upon us, or that we put upon ourselves, we begin to break out of the illusionary framework most of us are inevitably in.

We are more than what we can see with the naked eye. We are much more. We are essence, energy, vibrations that have been given a human form to explore an earthly life. Our souls are the guides on this journey and possess everything we need to enfold and embrace our lives here.

We have the power to be connected to everything, and to be non-attached to all things and outcomes. Remember, there is a difference between detached and non-attachment. When we form non-attachments, it simply means we are not attached to any outcome, whatever it may be, in whatever form.

We tend to attach feelings and emotions to outcomes. If X, Y, Z happens then everything will be okay, and I will then be happy and fulfilled. It's a myth and it's a lie. We are then waiting for certain external factors to be in place before we can *feel* a certain way. When these external factors are not in place, we get into our feelings and revert to victim mode.

WE ARE BLOODY AMAZING PEOPLE! We have at our disposal untapped power and unlimited potential to bring light and to set our authentic gifts free into the wider world. Our souls are yearning for us to break free from the status quo and create bigger paradigms for our lives and that of our fellow human beings, creating a better existence for us all.

Can you imagine what the world will be like when we all raise our levels of self-awareness and consciousness to come together? How magnificent and beautiful the world will be. Let us use this unique, omnipotent DNA we all possess.

~ P ~

Powerful

All the power we need to achieve anything here on earth lies within us. Energy is power and we are energy so, therefore, we are power. We can use our power for good, and this in turn creates in us even more power; we become powerful.

This inner force within us all is strong and yearns for us to take the time to pay attention, to acknowledge and to nurture its very being. Our soul, our inner self, becomes our very best friend, our soulmate, so to speak.

With every breath, we breathe new life. The breath is powerful in connecting all our senses to 'self'. We can then be fully present in the precise moment we are at.

This is power. This will centre our being, our presence, so we can be still and give time for our souls, our inner self, to respond.

This power comes from yielding and surrendering and allowing our souls, our inner self, to unfold and open up. This aids us in realizing and releasing our gifts to the wider realm of humanity. To share our souls. This is such a peaceful, beautiful and powerful experience. Some say this state is called bliss, and once you taste it, there is definitely no way you want to go back to existing through the status quo.

When we become aware – meaning being aware of our thought patterns, of our speech, of energy that surrounds us, of what we eat, the list can go on and on – we will bring about a powerful level of consciousness and *bliss* that will ultimately bring about powerful, intentional changes. It means, in general, paying attention, opening our 'conscious' eyes to really see more than what is presented to us. We all possess a limitless power of love and for good.

~ Q ~

Quintessential

Our inner selves, our souls, are the perfect representation of the Divine which has created us. We are all quintessentially unique. We are an exemplary embodiment of that which is from everlasting to everlasting. Of that which has no beginning, or no end. Our true selves typify all that surpasses all understanding and cannot be described or labelled. There is no definition of the essence of who we are. We simply are.

We are all modelled from the same source, the same energy, and we have been graced with the gift of representing that greater source, here on earth, at this time, right now. Our essence is here, as an epitome of that greater good. We are the embodiment of pure love, pure light.

We may have been blindsided along the way, with misinformation that has been imprinted and imparted on us, by family, friends, society at large, education, religion, etc. and this may cause us, momentarily, to forget who we truly are.

Being that our very breath, our soul DNA is already determined, and given the fact we are established from a highly quintessential source, we are encouraged that we can set our minds free from all that keeps us trapped in a mind that does not serve us.

We have the power and control to live beyond the perimeters of what is presented to us. We have the capabilities and the capacity to go beyond the status quo and to create a new *normal* all the time. Once we begin to tap into the well that is quintessentially a part of all of us, there really are no limits.

~ R ~

Release, Release, Release

We all need to learn how and develop the habit of letting go; to liberate, to release from our own minds and the constant over-chattering. When we begin to release, we realise it creates such a strong, beautiful and, also, a softer, lighter feeling within us. It creates a sense of inner peace. When we stop to inhale a breath, and a moment to release it, we can feel at ease, at balance.

Regularly taking moments to breathe, and breathe deeply, reconnects us to our inner self. It is a form of 'internal' communication, as opposed to having those moments in our head, where we will tell ourselves a thousand different stories, based on information that may or may not be true, and where we are undoubtedly attached to the emotions of an outcome.

When we begin to practise *non*-attachment to outcomes, we let ourselves free, we unchain ourselves. Remember, non-attachment is not the same as detachment. We become free by not attaching ourselves or identifying who we truly are by mere emotions, which are ever-changing. We are able to *feel* a feeling, embrace it, and release it without actually *becoming* the emotion, through response or reaction.

Instead, we can rest in balance, cushioned by a sense of inner bliss. True peace. This is the truth that truly sets us free, because we and we alone have total control of how we orchestrate our lives. Heaven and hell are not destination places our souls arrive at when we die. No, these are states of mental being; our present state of mind.

When we fully surrender to what is greater than us, and which exists within and without of us, that is when we arrive at our utopia.

~ S ~

Self-Love

Self-love entails that we stop looking around at all the 'stuff' that surrounds us, and take the time to see to our own personal self-care, in whichever way is right for us. This involves us completely switching off to unnecessary noises that like to take up residence in our minds.

Some of us will choose routes such as meditation and similar practices, to be still, silent, and to simply breathe. Communication with our inner selves. This can lead us to higher levels of consciousness when we take this time to simply be. Being with self.

Having a nice, hot bath, filled with bath salts and invigorating bath oils, or really appreciating having a hot shower, and being grateful for the water as it cleanses, can also be another way of showing some self-love.

Taking time out in the day to read a book that will help enhance well-being, a new hobby or learning a new skill like a language, or cooking a new style of cuisine, are ways we can express self-love.

When we care about ourselves, it does not mean that we are selfish. Quite the reverse. When we take care of ourselves fully, when we learn to truly love and appreciate the beings that we are. We are then in a place that can offer the world an authentic reflection of who we truly are, and generate higher vibrational levels of energy.

In turn, this energy produces the very best of who we are, and the gifts that we are all organically given can shine through, and we are then best able to share who we are, authentically, with those that we interact with, anytime, anywhere. Always authentic.

Self-care is such a beautiful experience. It helps us to connect to ourselves in a more holistic way, incorporating our minds, bodies and our souls: our essence. When our whole being sings off the same hymn sheet, we are then more equipped and aligned to join forces with all that is good and that surrounds us, and ultimately to the greatest energy source – the Divine Universe.

~ T ~

Trust in Truth

What is truth? Is it the absence of lies? Where is it within us, that rests and remains, this absence of lies?

Our very being is the only real truth. The 'being' within us has no concept of time or space. Its existence is not dependent on what we have, what we do not have, or where we were born or live. It makes no difference at all to where we were, or were not, educated, or how rich and famous we become. These eternal circumstances and situations make no difference to truth.

These external structures and life situations are ever-changing, ever-moving, evolving. Like feelings and emotions, there is no constant, no stay; forever shifting and fluctuating. So, for us to put our hopes, our faith, our core beliefs into these external, ever-changing limitations, is kind of crazy really, as these do not equate to the truth about who we really are and why we are here in existence.

Truth lies within us; deep, unchanging, forever rooted. Foundations that have been laid from the beginning of time. There resides our truth. When we commune and connect to this part of our inner selves, our internal satnav, we begin to rise above the level of consciousness we have for the most part been imprinted with; the false truths passed onwards to each generation, like an inheritance, that has no value, and in fact has accrued a lot of debt.

Like a smudged mirror, when we begin to wipe away the surface residue and clear away the marks, we begin to reveal the true nature of who we are and to comprehend the enormity of our very being, to appreciate what it is and what we are here to accomplish. Everything changes, except for one thing: the essence of who we are. Once we come to this level of realisation, we begin the journey anew, with our true self.

~ U ~

Unique

We all originate from the same source, and all share the same fundamental DNA, so to speak. However, in so saying, we are all unique, individual forms of life that have been granted the gift of experiencing life, here on earth, and each of us are equipped with varying, unique gifts and talents designed to help us along the way.

Our souls are rare, distinctive, and matchless in who we are, and each soul is exceptional in their authentic state. That is why we find that when we try to become someone or something we are inherently not, we lose sight of who we uniquely are, and may become unhappy, anxious, or feel a void within us that does not seem able to be filled.

Tapping into 'ourselves' and recognising our gifts is the start of great freedom. When we are instinctively drawn to create, in whatever form, it is our true nature releasing itself. Our true nature wants to step up, step out and experience this world as it should. Our true nature is creative at source, and our individuality allows us to do this beautifully.

When we engage in what we are naturally and authentically drawn to, we then get to experience life with a new level of enthusiasm. Let us celebrate who we naturally are, organically, authentically and genuinely, so we can experience life at the level we were intended to.

~ 𝒱 ~

Vibrantly Vital

Our very being is a ball of vibrant, energetic, pulsating luminosity. Our souls, our essence, have been given a human form to experience life on earth. This is a great blessing and gracious gift to us all, even if we may not realise or feel like this through certain points in our lifetime.

When we work with our inner vibrancy and begin to master the mind, which can become overcrowded with false truths and leave us feeling anxious and despondent, we can actively become more aware of our thoughts, our attachments to feelings and emotions and to their outcomes.

When we are aware, meaning when are minds are totally focused with the present moment, we are able to shift our level of consciousness, from a basic baseline to a more elevated level. Our vibrational energy heightens, we create new vital cells within our body and ultimately, we emit more energy, light and love.

We are all here for one reason or another. We were all destined to be here. No matter what is happening on the outside of us – that of our external situations and circumstances which, as we know, change frequently throughout our lifetime – remember we all have this vital vibrancy that encompasses our very being, and is more of who we are, and maybe more than we may ever truly know.

~ *W* ~

Wonderment

When we watch small children around us discover new things, we see their palpable sense of wonder and happiness, if they are engaging in some activity that brings them delight.

As adults, we tend to subdue this sense of wonderment of the world around us. Why and how do we become cynical, judgemental, and so conscious of just being? When do we lose this sense of wonder for the magic of life?

As we begin to grow older, we are conditioned into thinking and believing there is a certain pathway that our lives will have to take. Depending on where, when and the conditions we are born into, there will be vast differences to what story we will be told.

This makes life vastly capricious for us all, although we can change the narrative, so that we can all partake on a level playing field. We can achieve this by showing up as our authentic selves, without judgement of self or others. We can allow each of us to be fully who we are, allowing vulnerabilities to be exposed, so we can each help each other to become our highest form of self.

When we are enthusiastic about our lives and the lives of those around us, about the earth we inhabit, when we consciously open our hearts and minds to what is, we will begin to see the omnipotent wonder that surrounds us, and that is held within each one of us.

Let us develop a hunger to find out more about who we are, why we are here, and the planet we currently inhabit. Study like you are studying for an exam, a driving test, whatever it may be. We invest a lot of our time studying what is on social media, but to what end? Remember, we are the only true constant in our lifetime.

~ X ~

X-Ray

There are times that we need to self-examine and evaluate our responses and reactions to occurrences in our everyday life and, also, to incidences that occur in the wider world around us. Events and situations can sometimes provoke some form of reaction within us, that can cause us to become less than our best selves.

This 'X-ray' screening of self and of how we choose to respond to our external stimuli helps us to create a stronger bond with our inner self, as this is where all our answers undoubtedly lie. As we look more closely at our responses and reactions to life, amid and through the guidance of our inner self, we become more conscious and loving in our choices, responses and our reactions.

When we self-examine and use this X-ray vision to question our very selves, when we cut through all the external 'isms' that make us afraid and insecure, and through those mindsets and habits that hold us back from being authentic and true to who we are designed to be; when we cut through the fabric of the system and infrastructure that we inhabit; when we get to the core, it is here we find our light.

We can make this scanning of ourselves habitual in asking ourselves questions such as why do we respond to certain situations or individuals as we do? What is triggering this reaction from us? We then need to ask ourselves further questions, such as are we allowing imprinted teachings, opinions, past experiences and judgements to cloud our way of thinking and responding, not only to the world at large, but more importantly, to our own self?

If we want to change our external situations, we must retrain our minds to reflect that which we want to experience. Developing this X-ray vision into self allows us to expand our viewpoint on life and what it holds for us, and helps us to develop a higher level of consciousness.

~ 𝒴 ~

𝒴earn

To yearn is to have an intense feeling of longing for something. Innately, something that one has lost or been separated from. This yearning for us humans comes when our essence, our spirit self, calls for us to connect with our 'being' and that which is greater than us. That which is the true nature of who we are.

The reason why so many of us go about our lives in what seems to be a state of unconsciousness, or at the very best a basic level of consciousness, is that we have become accustomed to quieting our inner voice. This is brought about through the conditioning we experience after we are born into this world.

We have become dependent on those things that are external to us, to supply us with all the answers to the questions we have, and to fill all voids that we may feel we have in this life. Without a doubt, the world cannot give us every answer to every question, and neither can it ever fill every void with the 'things' of this world. The reason is that this 'yearning' we all feel at different junctions in our lives comes to us like a whisper, a nudge. Sometimes it may be a slight tap and, at other times, a big old slap. This is our inner voice, wanting and yearning for us to fully connect with self, and to empower us in who we truly are: powerful, intelligent, mindful beings.

So, just as we yearn for another to love and pour affection on, let us have that same level, even more so, for our own self. When we love and look after ourselves fully, we are then better equipped to be a greater force, and make a more positive impact, for those around us and, yes, for the greater good.

~ Z ~

Zeal

Go for it! Whatever 'it' is, go for it with vigour, enthusiasm, with zealous zeal! When we wake up in the morning, before our feet even touch the ground, let us develop the habit of giving thanks for the beautiful day we have been gifted, and begin it with an energy that shines bright (even if the sun isn't shining outside).

This zealous energy we encompass carries through, all through our body systems, body tissues and fibres, through our very cells, all the while sending messages to our brain. This powerful energy produces 'feelgood' natural chemicals within us, which the brain receives, and our bodies and minds react accordingly.

Remember, we first begin to 'feel' the way that we are thinking, then we begin to 'think' the way we feel. Just like a negative 'story' that we may tell ourselves, one that is infiltrated with non-truths we have become accustomed to believing. It starts as a tiny seed in the mind and, before you know it, has snowballed into a whole different saga altogether which, I may add, has solely been concocted in our own minds, through our own thoughts.

When we retrain our minds to operate with a certain sense of zealous enthusiasm, it enables us to be the best version of ourselves, not only for our own self, but for those around us, and the wider community. We emit a higher level of positive energy that in turn comes back to us, in all shapes and forms.

This zeal, this energy, is contagious, and once we have it, others will naturally be attracted to it. Some may come along, and may feel as though they are draining the natural resource of 'happy' energy we possess. No worries; this is when we step back and re-energise our being, in whichever way is best for us, and we can then come back, refreshed, refuelled and full of life-affirming ZEAL!

Thank You

In closing, I would firstly like to say a heartfelt thank you. Thank you for taking physical time and energy in reading this little book.

My intention here is that the context within this book will have touched you in some way and will have shown some insights into how we can use our own minds, and reclaim our inner power, to best navigate our journey through this wonderful world we all live in.

Do remember to be kind to yourself as you wander through this life, and ultimately, remember that you are love and loved.

Love and Light

Rosie x

About the Author

Rosemary, also affectionately known as 'Rosie', is a born-and-bred south Londoner. Her life over the years has taken many twists and turns, straight roads, and corners, which have ultimately brought her to a place where she now resides as her authentic 'self'.

During the time of the pandemic and lockdowns, we were gifted with a universal 'timeout', and Rosie took this opportunity to look at her life introspectively and began the process of holistically healing 'self', working on aspects of her mind, body and soul and arriving at a place of peace, freedom and blissful joy!

Rosie has discovered through her journey that the way to achieve true happiness is living an authentic life and always being true to oneself.

Conscious Dreams
PUBLISHING

Be the author of your own destiny

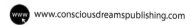
www.consciousdreamspublishing.com

info@consciousdreamspublishing.com

Let's connect